"*Mission Accomplished* by Scott James is a valuable resource for families. You and your children will be engaged by this devotional that shows the beautiful meaning of the Easter season. With activities, songs, discussion questions, and guided prayer times, James helps focus our hearts to appreciate all that Christ did for us in his death and resurrection."

JESSICA THOMPSON, Author *Exploring Grace Together*; frequent conference speaker

"Our hearts are often like a car out of alignment; when we take our hands off the wheel, it begins to swerve to the right or left. *Mission Accomplished* is a resource for the family to keep the affections of our heart aligned on the beauty of Christ leading up to Easter and far beyond. Theologically rich and incredibly practical, this is a fantastic resource for all families!"

JASON GASTON, Family Ministries Pastor, The Summit Church

"The approach of Easter gives families a distinctive opportunity to focus their devotional time on the purpose and implications of Jesus's atoning work. Scott James provides families with a concise and engaging two-week focus on the mission Jesus accomplished and the mission he is now calling us to for spreading the good news to the nations."

STEVE WATTERS, Editor of Council for Biblical Manhood and Womanhood's family channel; coauthor with Candice Watters of *Start Your Family: Inspiration for Having Babies*

"When it comes to leading spiritually in the home, the barrier for most parents is not a lack of desire, but a lack of equipping. That's why I'm thankful for *Mission Accomplished* by Scott H. James. In addition to helping parents teach their children about the resurrection of Christ and its implications for us, this devotional also gives parents on-the-job training on leading their families."

JOHN MURCHISON, Director of Children's Ministry, The Austin Stone Community Church

"*Mission Accomplished* is a fresh and inspiring presentation of the most Important Story featuring the Most Important Person who accomplished the most Important Rescue Mission on earth—the conquest of sin and death. Written in fourteen brief and creative segments, Scott offers families a meaningful and easy-to-use volume to consider and celebrate the Risen King together."

JOHN TICE, Children's Minister at The Church at Brook Hills; founder and president of Impress Kids

Mission Accomplished

A Two-Week Family
Easter Devotional

Scott James

Illustrated by A. E. Macha

New
Growth
Press

Mission
Accomplished

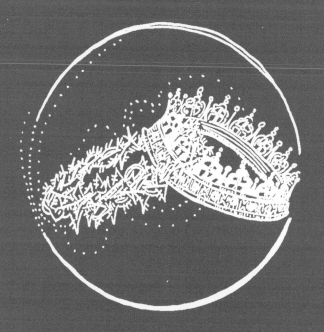

Scott James

Illustrated by A. E. Macha

New Growth Press, Greensboro, NC 27404
Copyright © 2015 by Scott James. All rights reserved.
Published 2015.

Scripture quotations are from The Holy Bible, English Standard Version®
(ESV®), copyright © 2001 by Crossway, a publishing ministry of Good News
Publishers. Used by permission. All rights reserved.

Cover Art: A. E. Macha
Cover/Interior Design and Typesetting: Faceout Books, faceoutstudio.com

ISBN: 978-1-939946-57-7 (Print)
ISBN: 978-1-939946-56-0 (eBook)

Library of Congress Cataloging-in-Publication Data

James, Scott, 1979-
 Mission accomplished : a two-week family devotional / Scott James.
    pages cm
 ISBN 978-1-939946-57-7 (print) -- ISBN 978-1-939946-56-0 (ebook) 1. Jesus
Christ--Passion--Prayers and devotions. 2. Families--Religious life. I. Title.
 BT431.3.J36 2015
 249--dc23
                          2014044428

Printed in United States of America

22 21 20 19 18 17 16 15   1 2 3 4 5

CONTENTS

Introduction

Nearly two thousand years ago, a wooden cross and an empty tomb served as the setting for the greatest rescue mission in history. Of course, this mission is none other than the gospel of Jesus Christ—the good news of a loving Father going to great lengths to save his broken children. The sad truth is that because we turned away from God and went our own way (Isaiah 53:6), each and every one of us has shattered our relationship with him. But the good news is that because of his compassion and mercy, God sent his very own Son on a mission of rescuing love to win us back. Every year at Easter, with a joyful shout of "Christ is risen!" we declare again the climax of this great story—Jesus has conquered sin and death! Although Easter Sunday comes only once a year, these truths should shape our lives every day.

The goal of these devotions is to help you lead your family in reflecting on Jesus's last days on earth and understanding the good news of his death, resurrection, and ascension. Starting on Palm Sunday, you'll spend two weeks walking with Jesus as he accomplished the mission his Father had given him. You will follow Jesus during the final days before his death, mourn with his followers as he is laid in the grave, and watch their fear give way to joy as they encounter the risen Lord. Then, you will see how God calls these same men and women on a Spirit-filled mission to spread the good news to the nations. Finally, you will consider together how God calls us to continue spreading the news of his gospel, promising us that his presence and power will fuel us as we go.

By going through the Easter story day-by-day, you and your children will be able to see how Jesus's death and resurrection are not far-off events that have no meaning for us, but are the basis for our daily life of faith and our confidence that our sins are forgiven and eternal life is ours. Just like adults, children struggle with guilt over the things they have done wrong, fears about death and judgment, and questions about their purpose in life. So as you read these devotions together, take the time to remind your children of the good news that their sins are forgiven, their future is assured, and they too have been given a mission from God to share the gospel with others.

How to Use This Book

For the week starting with Palm Sunday, you can use your Bible and these fourteen devotions as a framework for your family worship. Each devotion includes a Bible passage to read together, notes to help you discuss the passage with your child ("Think about It"), questions and answers to guide your discussion ("Talk about It"), and suggestions for a short time of prayer. Each devotional time could take anywhere from ten to twenty minutes.

Gathering together each day for a worship time will help communicate to your family that God is worth your time and attention. Family worship looks different in different households, so don't worry about whether or not you're doing it correctly. Simply focus on engaging your children with great and praiseworthy truths from God's Word. As an example, in my home we gather together at bedtime, sing a few hymns or praise songs, read and discuss a Bible passage, pray, and then close by singing the Doxology and reciting the Great Commission (Matthew 28:18–20). To keep it fresh, we incorporate a variety of other elements from time to time, including Scripture memorization, catechism questions, and a missionary prayer board. However you choose to do it, just keep it simple and engaging. This book is designed to help you read, understand, discuss, and pray through God's Word, so it should fit easily with a broad range of family worship formats. We've also included the lyrics to familiar hymns that you can sing together. In addition to the devotional material, we've provided activities that your family may enjoy doing together along the way.

Walking with
Jesus to the Cross

Do you remember everything you did last week? What did you have for lunch last Tuesday? What day was it that you started that new unit in math class? It's hard to remember everything that happened, right? Well, in these first seven devotions we will walk day by day with Jesus during the week leading up to a very important day. But how can we remember what he did two thousand years ago if we have trouble even remembering what we did last week? Thankfully, it's no mystery because Jesus's followers wrote it all down for us. So let's take a look at this important week in Jesus's life.

The King Has Come!

It's Palm Sunday and the King has come, just as God promised he would. Read about it in Luke 19:28–40.

Think about It

Jesus had a mission. As Passover week began, Jesus was heading into Jerusalem to do a very specific job—a job only he could do. Jesus's mission was to glorify God by rescuing his people from sin and bringing them back into God's family. Long ago, God created the very first man and woman, Adam and Eve, to be perfect—to love God and love each other. Sadly they decided to disobey God and do what they wanted instead of what God said would be best (Genesis 3). That's what the Bible calls sin. All the sad and bad things in the world started right then and there. Ever since, people have been running far away from God's loving care, thinking they would be happier doing things their own way. But they soon found out that life apart from God is not best. Disobeying God, they became lost and couldn't find their way back to him. Jesus came to give his life so that his lost people could be saved from sin and death and become God's children.

Jesus's mission wasn't a secret mission. God had been telling his people from the very beginning that a Rescuer would come (Genesis 3:15). Sure enough, Jesus came exactly as God promised he would, telling everyone that God was making a way for people to be reunited with him. As Jesus rode into Jerusalem to finish the most important part of the rescue plan, many recognized him as the saving King sent from God. They praised him and gave him a royal welcome. Some people didn't like that Jesus was being worshiped in this way. Jesus, however, told them that he deserves praise; in fact, if the people didn't praise him, the rocks themselves would cry out and give him glory!

Talk about It

○ Do you remember what happened in Israel's history that is celebrated at Passover (see Exodus 12)? Do you think it means anything that Jesus rode into Jerusalem as Passover week was starting? (*The Passover was when a spotless lamb died in place of Israel's firstborn sons. During this Passover celebration, Jesus, the Lamb of God, was coming to die in the place of sinful people. Just as God had rescued his people out of slavery in Egypt, he would now act to save them—to save us—from a different kind of slavery—slavery to sin.*)

○ Why was Jesus the only one qualified to carry out this rescue mission? *(The mission needed a perfectly sinless person to die as a punishment for other people's sin. Only God could live a perfectly holy life, but only a man could suffer and die a physical death. Jesus was uniquely qualified because he is fully God and fully man [Philippians 2:5-8].)*

○ Can you think of a time when you did something that showed how much you need to be rescued by Jesus too? *(Share with your child how Jesus rescued you. Encourage them to consider how they need to be rescued too.)*

Pray about It

Thank God for keeping his promise to send a Rescuer.

Sing about It

Praise to the Lord, the Almighty
Words by Joachim Neander

VERSE 1

Praise to the Lord, the Almighty, the King of creation!
O my soul, praise him, for he is thy health and salvation!
All ye who hear, now to his temple draw near,
Join me in glad adoration.

VERSE 2

Praise to the Lord, who o'er all things so wondrously reigneth,
Shelters thee under his wings, yea, so gently sustaineth!
Hast thou not seen how thy desires e'er have been
Granted in what he ordaineth?

VERSE 3

Praise to the Lord, who doth prosper thy work and defend thee!

Surely his goodness and mercy here daily attend thee.

Ponder anew what the Almighty will do,

If with his love he befriend thee.

VERSE 4

Praise to the Lord! O let all that is in me adore him!

All that hath life and breath, come now with praises before him!

Let the amen sound from his people again;

Gladly fore'er we adore him.

DAY 2

Sad
and Angry

Jesus weeps over the people who would reject
him and teaches about true worship. Read about it in
Luke 19:41-48 and Mark 11:17.

Think about It

Have you ever gotten a gift that you didn't appreciate at
first? Maybe you didn't know what it was; maybe you were
expecting something else?

Even though the people had just been shouting praises
to him, Jesus knew that many of them didn't truly understand his mission. Sadly, they couldn't see the gift they
had right in front of them. Just like when God freed Israel
from Egypt after the Passover, the people hoped Jesus
would free them from the Roman people who ruled over
them. The Israelites were more concerned about this than
they were about their sin and rebellion against God. Jesus

knew this and wept with sadness for those who would choose to overlook the kingdom of God.

Jesus then went into the temple—the House of God—and he did not like what he saw. The outer court of the temple was the one place where people could come and pray from all over the world (the inner part of the temple was just for the Jewish people). But the outer court was so full of people doing the business of the temple (exchanging money and selling the animals for sacrifice) that there was no room for the nations. God's plan had always been that the whole world would be blessed through Jesus (Genesis 12:2-3), but instead of welcoming the rest of the world, the money changers and those selling animals were making sure there was no room for them. Not only that, the place that was supposed to show a clear picture of God's greatness and holiness was full of cheaters and crooks. Jesus defended his Father's name and made room for the Gentiles by running these people out of the temple.

As Jesus taught about what it means to have a true relationship with God, the angry religious leaders began to think about how they could get rid of Jesus. They were not interested in hearing about how they needed to be rescued.

Talk about It

○ When he was thinking about being rejected by the people, does it surprise you that Jesus was sad enough to cry? *(Parents, discuss with your children that Jesus is merciful and compassionate, desiring that all people would trust in him and be saved.)*

○ Why was Jesus so angry with the salesmen in the temple? *(Jesus was angry because there was no room for the people he came to save and because instead of worshiping God, the people in the temple were just interested in making money.)*

Pray about It

Ask God to give you a heart of compassion and love for the lost.

Family Activity

PAINT THE PRAISES

When Jesus entered Jerusalem, he said that if the people didn't praise him then the very stones would cry out (Luke 19:40). Gather some rocks and paint praises on them such as "Hosanna!" "Blessed is he!" and "Praise the Lord!" Talk about how all of creation sings God's praise!

Teaching in the Temple

Jesus predicts his death and warns those who refuse God's rescue plan. Read about it in Luke 20:9-18.

Think about It

Jesus told a story about some men who were taking care of another person's vineyard. These men wanted to keep all the grapes from the vineyard without having to answer to the farm's owner. When Jesus told stories like this, the characters often represented other people. Can you guess who the characters point to in this story?

Just as the tenants beat up the owner's messengers and killed his son, the religious leaders of Israel had a long history of rejecting God's messengers. In fact, they would soon kill God's very own Son, Jesus. They would refuse God's rescue plan—his beloved Son—and would therefore face God's judgment.

This story helps us to remember that God alone can save. We all need to be rescued from sin, but any human plan for accomplishing this goes against God's plan. The religious leaders Jesus was talking to had rejected God's plan for saving Israel. Instead of listening to God's beloved Son, they wanted to go their own way and stay in charge, but Jesus told them that the Son they were rejecting would be the one who brings salvation for all people. The "stone the builders rejected" (Jesus) would become the cornerstone of the new people of God. After Jesus's death, God's people would be all who believed in Jesus, no matter what their nationality or race.

Talk about It

○ What does Jesus mean in verse 16 when he says in the story that the vineyard would be given to others? *(It means that salvation would not belong to Israel alone. People from every nation would be included in the kingdom of God.)*

○ Why were the religious leaders so upset when Jesus said this? *(This upset them because they were proud that they were God's chosen people and did not want to share this privilege with others.)*

○ How are we like the tenants in this parable? (*Without the Spirit of God working in our hearts, we will also reject Jesus and his plan to rescue us. Just like the tenants, we too are naturally God's enemies, but that doesn't stop God from loving us and sending Jesus to die for us [Romans 5:10].*)

Pray about It

Thank God that he has made salvation available for people of every nation.

Sing about It

The Church's One Foundation

Words by Samuel J. Stone

VERSE 1

The church's one foundation is Jesus Christ, her Lord;
She is his new creation by water and the Word:
From heav'n he came and sought her to be his holy bride;
With his own blood he bought her, and for her life he died.

VERSE 2

Elect from ev'ry nation, yet one o'er all the earth,
Her charter of salvation, one Lord, one faith, one birth;
One holy name she blesses, partakes one holy food,
And to one hope she presses, with ev'ry grace endued.

VERSE 3

'Mid toil and tribulation, and tumult of her war,
She waits the consummation of peace forevermore;
Till with the vision glorious, her longing eyes are blest,
And the great church victorious shall be the church at rest.

A Different Kind of King

Jesus was not the kind of king the people expected or wanted. Read about it in Luke 21:20-28.

Think about It

Can you imagine the mightiest king on earth? The people of Israel hoped Jesus would be a great king who would build them into a powerful nation once again, but Jesus taught them that their expectations were much too small. Jesus wanted to show the people that he was even better than that! Yes, Jesus was the king Israel had been waiting for, but he was a different kind of king than they expected. He showed them that lasting salvation couldn't be found in human kingdoms—they will all pass away.

Jerusalem was Israel's greatest and most beloved city, but Jesus told a terrifying story of an enemy attack that would destroy it. The message was clear: don't put your hope in this place. Human kingdoms are here today and gone tomorrow, but the kingdom of God stands forever. Even as Jesus was planning on going to the cross to rescue us from our sin, he wanted us to know that he was doing it in a way that would last *for all time*. Jesus wasn't only talking about the destruction of Jerusalem in this passage. He was also talking about when he would come again at the end of the world. On that Last Day, King Jesus will appear from above with power and great glory to bring his followers into God's kingdom forever. *That* is what we should put our hope in.

This passage is not just a warning to the people of Jesus's day. It is also a warning to us of what will happen if we don't trust in Jesus for forgiveness of our sins. One day every person will have to give an account to God for what he or she has done. God can accept nothing less than perfection, because he is perfect and that's what his law requires (Matthew 5:48). Jesus was warning the people of his day because he cared for them. He also cares for us and wants us to turn to him to be saved. If we trust in Jesus, instead of being afraid to meet God on Judgment Day, we will point to Jesus and say, "He paid for my sins on the cross." And our heavenly Father will open his arms wide to welcome us into his family where we will live forever (Hebrews 9:27–28).

Talk about It

○ Why do you think God allowed Jerusalem to be destroyed? *(Jerusalem was destroyed forty years after Jesus spoke these words both as a judgment for sin and because the destruction of Jerusalem meant the end of sacrifices in the temple. Jesus's death and resurrection meant that those sacrifices were no longer needed [Hebrews 10:10-14]. God's Word also warns us that a final judgment will come on the Last Day when Jesus returns.)*

○ Why do you think Jesus warned the people about God's judgment? *(Jesus warned the people because he loved them and wanted them to come to him in faith so they could be rescued. And many were rescued. See Acts 2 for the story of how many people, even those who wanted him crucified, put their faith in Jesus.)*

○ As we prepare to celebrate Easter, how should we think about the second coming of Jesus? *(As believers, we should look forward to that day in hope because Jesus has paid for our sins. We are forgiven and our salvation will be made complete—we will be glorified with God in heaven, forever free from sin. Also, knowing that unbelievers will receive final judgment for their sin on that day should cause us to live with urgency as we share the love of Jesus with them.)*

Pray about It

Ask God to help you live in joyful anticipation of Jesus's second coming.

Family Activity

TWO CROWNS

Draw two crowns: the one people thought Jesus would wear, and the one he wore the day he was crucified. (If you need help, read John 19:1-5).

The Two Cups

The cup of salvation and the cup of God's anger—
read about them in Luke 22:14-23, 39-44.

Think about It

As he gathered with his disciples to celebrate the Passover meal, Jesus showed them that he was the true Passover Lamb. Just as the innocent lamb died in place of the first-born sons of Israel, Jesus's mission of love would lead him to give his life in place of God's rebellious people. His body would be broken and his blood poured out for us. Jesus's sacrifice would be the start of the new covenant, or promise, from God, pictured as a cup holding the blood that he would shed for us. This cup reminds us that God, by his grace, will save sinners who trust in Christ alone.

Have you ever had to do something that you knew would be painful, but totally worth it in the end? Jesus had to do something like this, but so much harder than anything we will ever face. After eating the Passover meal, Jesus went out to pray in a garden. He knew what was ahead of him and was ready to go through with it, but that didn't mean it was easy. In order for Jesus to accomplish his rescue mission, he knew that he would have to take the penalty for our disobedience to God. This meant that he would become the target for all of God's wrath—God's holy anger toward sin. To bless us with the cup of the new covenant, Jesus would take the painful cup of wrath. Every sinner deserves to be punished for sin, but Jesus would step in and take our place instead.

Talk about It

○ What does Jesus mean when he says in Luke 22:22 that he will go "as it has been determined"? *(Jesus's sacrificial death would happen according to the purpose and plan of God.)*

○ Why did Jesus have to suffer the wrath of God? Why couldn't God just overlook our sin? *(God is holy and just. He will not let sin go unpunished because that would be unjust.)*

○ When you ask God to forgive you for something you did wrong, how can you know for sure that you will be forgiven? *(Because Jesus took the cup of God's wrath for us, we can be sure that God's anger won't be poured out on us. When we confess our sins, we can be certain that we are forgiven because of what Jesus did for us on the cross [see 1 John 1:9-10].)*

Pray about It

Thank Jesus for suffering the wrath that we deserve.

Sing about It

There Is a Fountain Filled with Blood
Words by William Cowper

VERSE 1

There is a fountain filled with blood, drawn from Immanuel's veins;
And sinners, plunged beneath that flood, lose all their guilty stains:
Lose all their guilty stains, lose all their guilty stains;
And sinners plunged beneath that flood, lose all their guilty stains.

VERSE 2

The dying thief rejoiced to see that fountain in his day;
And there have I, though vile as he, washed all my sins away:
Washed all my sins away, washed all my sins away;
And there have I, though vile as he, washed all my sins away.

VERSE 3

E'er since by faith I saw the stream your flowing wounds supply,
Redeeming love has been my theme, and shall be till I die:
And shall be till I die, and shall be till I die;
Redeeming love has been my theme, and shall be till I die.

VERSE 4

Dear dying Lamb, your precious blood shall never lose its pow'r,
Till all the ransomed church of God be saved to sin no more:
Be saved to sin no more, be saved to sin no more;
Till all the ransomed church of God be saved to sin no more.

The Most Important Day in History

Jesus dies on the cross as a punishment for our sin.
Read about it in Luke 23:32-47.

Think about It

Have you ever been surprised with a gift that you know you didn't really deserve? On the cross, God has given us the most undeserved gift ever! The penalty for sin is death. Although Jesus had lived a life without sin, he willingly took that penalty on himself when he hung on the cross. By doing this, Jesus provided the only way for us to be brought back to the Father. When we trust in Jesus, God forgives our sin and gives us the credit for Jesus's perfect life.

The criminals on the two crosses next to Jesus show us that Jesus is ready to save anyone who has faith in him. One criminal refused to believe Jesus and remained separated from God, but the other criminal saw who Jesus really was and trusted in him as his Rescuer. Though guilty, this man received more than he could imagine—he was brought into God's family forever.

By carrying out his mission on this one day, Jesus changed everything in the world. Nearly two thousand years later, his death *still* has the power to save us from our sin!

Talk about It

○ Was Jesus powerful enough to fight back and free himself from the cross? Why do you think he didn't? *(Jesus was powerful enough to free himself, but he didn't because he wasn't worried about protecting himself; he was acting to save his people by sacrificing himself. Though innocent, he didn't fight against his death because it was part of the mission he came to accomplish.)*

○ What did the Roman soldier who saw Jesus's death think afterward (Luke 23:47)? *(Based on what Jesus said and did as he was crucified, the soldier thought that Jesus must have been innocent ["righteous" NIV]. Righteous means that you do everything right. The Roman soldier might not have realized it, but what he said about Jesus was true—the one person in the world who did everything right was crucified for all the wrong things we have done.)*

Pray about It

Thank God for dying in our place so that we could be brought back to him.

Family Activity

DISPLAY THE CROSS

Gather two sticks from the yard and tie them together into a cross using twine or rope. You can use the cross to review the events of the week by draping it with a purple cloth (signifying our repentance) when recalling events from Palm Sunday through Maundy Thursday, changing the drape to a black cloth (commemorating Jesus's death) on Good Friday, and finally replacing it with a white cloth (symbolizing the resurrection) on Easter morning.

The Dark Day in Between

Jesus is dead in the grave.
Read about it in Luke 23:50-56.

Think about It

We tend to look back at Jesus's death and focus on how great a thing it was (and it was!). But we should also remember that to his disciples, Jesus's death was a frightening thing. Imagine having the thing you want most in life right in front of you, and then having it taken away. Would you feel disappointed? Confused? Crushed? Jesus, the one in whom these disciples had put all of their trust, was dead and buried. They had believed Jesus would be the one to rescue them! All hope appeared to be lost.

Before he died, Jesus had often told his disciples about the details of his rescue mission—that he would suffer, die, and then rise to life again (Luke 9:22). Now that Jesus was dead, these words must have been hard for the disciples to remember because they began to be filled with doubt. Had Jesus really been the savior they were waiting for? Were they wrong to trust in him?

Talk about It

○ Can you think of a time when bad things happening around you made it difficult to believe that God had a good plan for you? *(Parents, open up with your children about how sometimes it can be hard to see how God is working through trials and tribulations, but that we can always trust that he is acting for our good and for his glory, just like when he used Jesus's death to save his people.)*

○ Have you ever had trouble believing that someone would keep a promise? How is God different than other people who make promises? *(People will often let us down, but God is the perfect promise keeper. He will always do what he says [Numbers 23:19])*

Pray about It

Ask God to help you overcome fear and doubt by trusting in his promises.

Sing about It

When I Survey the Wondrous Cross

Words by Isaac Watts

VERSE 1

When I survey the wondrous cross
On which the Prince of glory died,
My richest gain I count but loss,
And pour contempt on all my pride.

VERSE 2

Forbid it, Lord, that I should boast,
Save in the death of Christ my God;
All the vain things that charm me most,
I sacrifice them to his blood.

VERSE 3

See, from his head, his hands, his feet,
Sorrow and love flow mingled down;
Did e'er such love and sorrow meet,
Or thorns compose so rich a crown?

VERSE 4

Were the whole realm of nature mine,
That were a present far too small;
Love so amazing, so divine,
Demands my soul, my life, my all.

The Risen King

Have you ever noticed that really good stories usually have some sad parts near the end when everything seems to be falling apart with no happy ending in sight? Then, right when all seems lost, something wonderful happens and everything is made right. Well, God is the best storyteller of all, and the amazing part is that his stories are true! Right now, we've reached the part of God's story where things seem like they've gone wrong—that Jesus's rescue mission has failed. But this week we will see that God has something wonderful in store for his people. As in any good story, the light shines brightest after you've come out of the dark.

Death
Is Defeated

Jesus rises from the grave, proving that he is the true Savior. Read about it in Luke 24:1–12.

Think about It

The women who visited the tomb on Sunday morning took spices with them so that they could finally prepare Jesus's body for burial. They had not been able to do it the day before because it was the Sabbath—the day of rest. The women expected to find a lifeless, stinky body but instead they found an empty tomb and two glorious angels who told them something amazing: "Why do you seek the living among the dead? He is not here, but has risen" (Luke 24:5–6). These words announced the wonderful truth that the grave could not hold Jesus. He had defeated death itself!

Have you ever wanted to buy something but not had enough money to pay for it? Unless you're able to pay the full price you can't have it, can you? Well, Jesus died to pay the full penalty for sin, and by raising him from the dead God showed that he had accepted Jesus's death as full payment. When Jesus died in our place, God declared that it was the *full* and *final* payment for sin. Those who trust in Jesus don't have to pay for their own sins. Just like a well-known hymn says, "Jesus paid it all." In another part of the Bible, God also tells us that Jesus's resurrection proved he is the Son of God, the promised Savior (Romans 1:2-4). The angel at the empty tomb reminded the women that all this happened exactly as Jesus said it would. Just as it had been planned from the very beginning, God came down on a mission to save his people.

Talk about It

○ In this passage, the disciples didn't believe that Jesus had risen from the dead when they first heard the news. Is it surprising to you that they found it hard to believe? *(Parents, help your children appreciate just how astounding this news was. Sometimes we can take the resurrection for granted because we are so used to hearing about it. Take some time to marvel at the resurrection with your children.)*

○ Even though the resurrection was astonishing, why should the disciples not have been completely surprised by it? *(The disciples should not have been completely surprised because Jesus had told them that it was the plan all along! The disciples failed to remember and trust in Jesus's words.)*

Pray about It

Praise God for crushing death through the resurrection of his Son, Jesus.

Sing about It

Christ the Lord Is Risen Today

Words by Charles Wesley

VERSE 1

"Christ, the Lord, is ris'n today," Alleluia!
Sons of men and angels say; Alleluia!
Raise your joys and triumphs high; Alleluia!
Sing, ye heav'ns, and earth, reply, Alleluia!

VERSE 2

Lives again our glorious King, Alleluia!
Where, O death, is now thy sting? Alleluia!
Dying once he all doth save, Alleluia!
Where thy victory, O grave? Alleluia!

VERSE 3

Love's redeeming work is done, Alleluia!
Fought the fight, the battle won, Alleluia!
Death in vain forbids him rise, Alleluia!
Christ hath opened Paradise, Alleluia!

VERSE 4

Soar we now where Christ has led, Alleluia!
Foll'wing our exalted Head, Alleluia!
Made like him, like him we rise, Alleluia!
Ours the cross, the grave, the skies, Alleluia!

All Scripture Points to Him

Something happens to two disciples on a walk to Emmaus. Read about it in Luke 24:13-27.

Think about It

Has anyone ever told you something that was hard to believe? What was it? The disciples had seen the empty tomb, but they were still not sure what to believe. They had been reminded that Jesus himself had told them this would happen, but could it really be true? During a walk to a neighboring town, two of Jesus's disciples were discussing these things when Jesus himself came alongside and joined in the conversation. But he hid who he was from them so that they wouldn't recognize him. I bet you didn't know that Jesus went on undercover missions too, did you? Because Jesus is God, he didn't have to wear a disguise, he just made their eyes see him differently. Jesus did this so that he could talk with them and help them understand the truth behind everything that was happening.

Jesus read through the Scriptures with the men, pointing out that the Savior's death wasn't an unexpected twist in the story—God's message had always been that we need to be rescued and that he would accomplish it in this way. Jesus showed them that it was God's plan all along for the Rescuer to suffer for his people before finishing his mission and returning to heaven.

Talk about It

- When Jesus died, did God need to come up with a back-up plan to finish the rescue mission? *(No, Jesus willingly gave up his life because that was the plan—the only plan—all along.)*

- What do you think Jesus meant in Luke 24:26 when he said he was entering into his glory? *(He was talking specifically about his resurrection, but he may also have been pointing forward to when he would ascend back into heaven.)*

Pray about It

Thank God for revealing himself and his rescue plan in his Word.

Family Activity

IMAGINE THE RESURRECTION!

Have everyone create a picture that represents Jesus's resurrection. Use any media that you desire (e.g., crayons, markers, paints, cut paper). It can be realistic or abstract. Display the finished creations.

Ghosts Don't Eat

A risen Jesus appears to the disciples.
Read about it in Luke 24:36-49.

Think about It

Jesus's closest disciples gathered together, still full of fear and doubts. They had heard the reports of the risen Lord but had not yet seen him with their own eyes. All of a sudden, Jesus appeared in the middle of the room and invited them to touch and see that he really was alive. He gave them real proof that his body had been raised from the dead—he was no ghost or vision. He even sat down and ate some fish with them! When was the last time you passed the salt to a man who had been buried in a graveyard the day before? Can you imagine what the disciples must have been thinking?

It's interesting that Jesus didn't get upset with his disciples for needing so much proof to believe that he was really alive. He patiently gave them the evidence they needed so that they could understand what had happened. Now that they saw that the promises written about him had come true, Jesus called his disciples to carry on his mission by sharing the good news of salvation with everyone around. Because of what they had seen and heard from the risen Savior, they couldn't help themselves—they just had to tell the good news to everyone!

Talk about It

○ Faith means putting our hope and trust in something that we can't see with our physical eyes (Hebrews 11:1). Does this mean we should ignore facts and evidence completely? (No, Jesus shows us here that evidence of the truth is a good thing. In the end, though, we are called to trust God whether or not we think we have enough proof.)

○ After the disciples saw Jesus alive after his crucifixion, Jesus called them to be witnesses of what happened and to tell others the good news of forgiveness for sins. Did Jesus leave them to do this in their own power? (No, he said that he would send the promise of the Father to give them power from God. This points to the coming of the Holy Spirit.)

Pray about It

Ask God to fill you with faith so you too can be a witness to others who don't know Jesus—to those who haven't heard that their sins can be forgiven and they can live forever with God.

Sing about It

'Tis So Sweet to Trust in Jesus
Words by Louisa M. R. Stead

VERSE 1

'Tis so sweet to trust in Jesus,
Just to take him at his word;
Just to rest upon his promise,
Just to know, "Thus saith the Lord!"

REFRAIN

Jesus, Jesus, how I trust him!
How I've proved him o'er and o'er!
Jesus, Jesus, precious Jesus!
O for grace to trust him more!

VERSE 2

O how sweet to trust in Jesus,
Just to trust his cleansing blood;
Just in simple faith to plunge me
'Neath the healing, cleansing flood!

VERSE 3

Yes, 'tis sweet to trust in Jesus,
Just from sin and self to cease;
Just from Jesus simply taking
Life and rest, and joy and peace.

VERSE 4

I'm so glad I learned to trust him,
Precious Jesus, Savior, Friend;
And I know that thou art with me,
Wilt be with me to the end.

Marching Orders

Fueled by Jesus's power and presence, we are called by him to make disciples of all nations. Read about it in Matthew 28:16–20.

Think about It

If you knew that what you were saying would be one of the last things you'd be able to say face-to-face to your friends, you'd want to make sure that your words were important, right?

Soon, Jesus's mission on earth would be over and he would return to his Father in heaven. Before he went, he brought his disciples together on a mountainside to give them their final marching orders. The words Jesus said here are so important that even though they were spoken a long time ago, they are still true for all followers of Jesus today. We call them the "Great Commission."

Jesus accomplished his great rescue plan and now he sends us out as messengers of the good news. Just like a great commander would send out troops on a special assignment, Jesus has sent us on a mission to bring glory to God by making disciples of all nations. This means that as we live for Jesus, we call others to know, love, and follow him as well. We tell people that even though they have disobeyed God, they can be rescued. Every believer is called to be a part of this amazing mission. It seems like it's too big of a job for us to do, but Jesus promises that he will be with us as we go. That's good news because *nothing* is too difficult for him.

Talk about It

○ How can Jesus claim to have ALL authority in heaven and on earth? Is he exaggerating? *(No, Jesus has absolute power over all things because he is God.)*

○ As they go out to make disciples, what are they to do? *(They are to baptize those who trust in Jesus so that they are identified with Jesus and his followers, and then teach them to become like Jesus as they learn to obey everything Jesus told his disciples.)*

○ What promise did Jesus make to his disciples (and to us) along with his directions? *(He will be with his disciples from the beginning to the end.)*

Pray about It

Ask God to give you confidence in his presence and dependence on his power as you seek to make disciples of all nations.

Family Activity

CARRY OUT THE MISSION

Be intentional about obeying the Great Commission together as a family by looking for opportunities to serve your community. As you do, trust in the Spirit to give you opportunities to share the good news of Jesus Christ. Some possibilities include:

○ Help a neighbor who is in need of yard work or some other small project around the home.

○ Practice hospitality by inviting others into your home for fellowship and a meal.

○ Reach "all nations" by engaging cross-cultural populations in and around your community. Begin by asking your local church about outreach ministries toward the least-reached people groups in your area and pray about how your family can join in on mission.

Consider making this a family tradition every Easter, continuing to build these relationships all year long.

DAY 12

Jesus Returns Home

The King rises to his heavenly throne.
Read about it in Acts 1:1-11.

Think about It

After his resurrection, Jesus stayed with his disciples for forty days and taught them about the kingdom of God. Hundreds of people saw him during this time—there were eyewitnesses to his resurrection everywhere! Jesus was preparing his disciples to carry the good news of the great rescue all over the world, but he knew that this mission was too big for them to do on their own. He encouraged the disciples by reminding them that God is in control and by promising them that the Holy Spirit would give them power to be bold witnesses for him.

After he promised his followers that the Spirit would come, Jesus rose up into the sky and was taken back into heaven.

Can you imagine what that would be like? One minute you're standing there talking to him and the next minute he's soaring up into the clouds! Right now, Jesus is seated on his throne with God the Father, where he rules over everything with great power and authority. On the Last Day, he will come back down in the same way that he went up. On that great day, he will bring the salvation of his people to completion. The next time you see a beautiful cloud with the sun shining through it, imagine how amazing it would be to see Jesus floating down from it. Praise God that we get to look forward to this!

Talk about It

o Why was the coming of the Holy Spirit so important to our mission? *(Because no matter how good we are at telling people about Jesus, it is ultimately the work of God that convicts people of sin and convinces them of their need for a Savior.)*

o How does it make you feel to know that Jesus is ruling in heaven as the King of kings? *(Parents, talk with your children about the great confidence we have in knowing that our Lord reigns over all things [see Colossians 1:15-17].)*

Pray about It

Praise Jesus as the King of all creation.

Sing about It

Crown Him with Many Crowns

Words by Matthew Bridges (verses 1, 3, 4)
and Godfrey Thring (verse 2)

VERSE 1

Crown him with many crowns, the Lamb upon his throne;
Hark! how the heav'nly anthem drowns all music but its own:
Awake, my soul, and sing of him who died for thee,
And hail him as thy matchless King through all eternity.

VERSE 2

Crown him the Lord of life, who triumphed o'er the grave,
And rose victorious in the strife for those he came to save;
His glories now we sing who died, and rose on high,
Who died eternal life to bring, and lives that death may die.

VERSE 3

Crown him the Lord of peace, whose pow'r a scepter sways
From pole to pole, that wars may cease, absorbed in prayer
and praise:
His reign shall know no end; and round his pierced feet
Fair flow'rs of paradise extend their fragrance ever sweet.

VERSE 4

Crown him the Lord of love; behold his hands and side,
Rich wounds, yet visible above, in beauty glorified:
All hail, Redeemer, hail! For Thou hast died for me:
Thy praise shall never, never fail throughout eternity.

A New Life

Those who belong to Jesus live with resurrection power!
Read about it in Romans 6:1-14. This somewhat
difficult passage can be read from a version like the
New International Reader's Version or *The Message*
to make it easier to understand.

Think about It

When we trust in Jesus to rescue us from sin, our lives
become joined with him. This means that our old life that
was trapped in sin has been done away with and we have
been given a new life in Jesus. Just like Jesus's resurrection
showed that death had no power over him, sin has no final
power over us in our new Spirit-filled lives. Praise God he
has brought us from death to life!

Since sin no longer controls us, it would be silly to
continue obeying it instead of God. Sin is not the boss of us
anymore—we have a great new boss who has accomplished
his mission by freeing us from sin. If you were freed from
a jail cell you'd been locked up in for a long time, do you
think it would make much sense to turn around and run back

behind the bars? No, you'd run far away from the jail! So it is with sin—in Christ, we are free to run far from it! Because we are one with Jesus, we can grow to be more like him as we confidently live in the power of his life, trusting in his promise that one day he will get rid of sin entirely. This doesn't mean that it isn't a fight to turn away from our sins, but it does mean that we have the power of God on our side now. Because we have the Spirit of God living inside us, we can say No! to sin. And because Jesus died on the cross, when we do sin, we can go to him for forgiveness and know that no matter what we have done God will forgive us because of Jesus's death on the cross (1 John 1:9–10).

Talk about It

○ How does it feel to know that those who believe in Jesus are no longer slaves to sin? *(Sometimes we can trick ourselves into thinking that sin is unavoidable, but this isn't true. In Christ, we are free to refuse sin and do what is right. Remember the two greatest commands are to love God and to love others—love is always the best way to do the right thing [Matthew 22:36-40].)*

○ The end of Romans 6:14 says that we are not under law but under grace. What do you think this means? *(Under God's law, we deserve death for our sin. In God's grace, Jesus forgives our sin because he has already paid the penalty for it. The blessing of grace means that no matter what sins we commit, there is now no condemnation for those who are in Christ Jesus [see Romans 8:1].)*

Pray about It

Thank God for making a way for us to be free from the power of sin.

Family Activity

SPROUT TO NEW LIFE

Fill a clear plastic cup with soil. Place a couple of seeds in the cup and lightly cover them with soil. Then watch them grow. Beans, if soaked in water for a day, sprout quickly, sometimes within three or four days. Flowers such as marigolds, zinnias, and sunflowers also sprout quickly. As you watch the new shoots grow, talk about how the seed itself dies in order to sprout new life, just as Christ died so that we may have new life in him. Read John 12:24 together.

DAY 14

Living with Hope

Those who trust in Jesus live in eager anticipation of his return. Read about it in Philippians 3:17–21.

Think about It

It's hard to be happy about having to wait for something, even if we know it'll be great, isn't it? Remember that Christmas gift that arrived early and sat under the tree for two weeks?

What do we look forward to? Are we more excited by the cool things we see around us today or by the glorious future that God has promised us? Followers of Jesus are waiting for something truly amazing; we have been brought into God's family and are told to look forward to the best family reunion ever. This reunion will happen in God's kingdom, but this kingdom is not a place on a map that you can drive to.

We can see some of this kingdom on earth now, anywhere God's people live under his good rule, enjoying his presence. But we are waiting for the day when God will remake the entire world into his eternal kingdom. In the meantime, part of our mission is to remember that our true home is not here on earth, but in heaven. Jesus has gone to prepare a place for us, but he has promised that he will come back on the Last Day to bring his people into the kingdom for good. Amazingly, God says he will make our bodies into glorious and sinless bodies that will last forever. With all of this to look forward to, followers of Jesus aren't caught up with only earthly things; we look to heaven, waiting with great hope for the day of his return. Knowing that God has already come down on a mission of love to rescue us from sin, we can hope for that return with great confidence.

Talk about It

○ Where can we see glimpses of God's kingdom here on earth? *(We can see glimpses of God's kingdom in the lives of believers who have committed their lives to Jesus and who live according to his Word. We should see this most clearly in the church.)*

○ How does looking forward to Jesus's return affect the way we live today? *(Joyful anticipation of his second coming can fuel our desire to live for the glory of God every day. It should also give us a sense of urgency when it comes to sharing Jesus with people who do not know him.)*

Pray about It

Ask God to give you an eternal outlook that affects the way you live every day.

Sing about It

On Jordan's Stormy Banks
Words by Samuel Stennett

VERSE 1

On Jordan's stormy banks I stand
And cast a wishful eye
To Canaan's fair and happy land,
Where my possessions lie.

VERSE 2

All o'er those wide extended plains
Shines one eternal day;
There God the Son forever reigns
And scatters night away.

VERSE 3

No chilling winds nor pois'nous breath
Can reach that healthful shore;
Sickness and sorrow, pain and death
Are felt and feared no more.

VERSE 4

When shall I reach that happy place
And be forever blest?

When shall I see my Father's face
And in his bosom rest?

CHORUS
I am bound for the promised land,
I am bound for the promised land;
O who will come and go with me?
I am bound for the promised land.